The Many *Apparels of* WOMEN

The Many Hats We Wear

By Maxine Henry

PRESS

The Many Apparels of Women
The Many Hats We Wear
by Maxine Henry

Printed in the United States of America.

ISBN 9781498452601

Unless otherwise indicated, Scripture is taken from the King James Version of the Bible.

Scripture marked NIV is taken from the HOLY BIBLE, NEW INTERNATIONAL VERSION®. NIV®. Copyright © 1973, 1978, 1984 by International Bible Society. Used by permission of Zondervan. All rights reserved.

www.xulonpress.com

ACKNOWLEDGEMENTS

F irst, I thank God for the initiative and opportunity to write this book. Secondly to my loving late husband, Charles Henry, Jr., who so graciously supported me throughout all my efforts to produce the training, and as a result, "The Many Apparels of Women's Book." Charles was ill most of that time, but encouraged me, by financially supporting the conference. His liberality and understanding helped me to move forward with my plans. He truly wanted to see that my efforts were successful. To my daughter, Wanda, my niece, Ebony, and all my godchildren who supported my vision. Also, to all the local church ladies and those participants who offered their support. Special thanks to my State Supervisor, Mother Mable Gibbons. She encouraged me and pursued permission of our Jurisdictional Prelate, of the state of Alaska, Churches of God in Christ; to sanction the conference as a State function for the Women's Department. My grateful appreciation to Bishop C.D. Williams for granting me the permission and privilege to work with the women of the State for ten consecutive years, in effort to expand our knowledge through training for outreach ministries.

Many sisters had an opportunity to fellowship with other Christian women groups in our community, and eventually from the lower 48 states. The conferences lasted for ten years with continual growth. Many hearts and souls were blessed throughout the duration of the outreach ministries. These conferences were very much in line with the C.O.G.I.C. Urban Initiatives being implemented today.

My gratitude to all the women in the Northern District, from Fairbanks and North Pole, Alaska, who supported and participated in the conferences. There are many others, who played an intricate role in the accomplishments. I will forever remember, the late Sister Phyllis Webb, who worked so faithfully with me each year, along with her daughters. They graciously put together the Conference materials for each event. Also, Evangelist Frances Avery-Stoute, who ***demonstrated. Hats, Hats, Hats, at the first conference which was a true reflection of my vision*** and the conference theme.

Special thanks to the out-of-state guest and speakers: Dr. Vivian Wesson, Memphis, TN; Mother Ruby Dubose, Harvey, IL; Evangelist Sandra Byrd, Charlotte, NC; Evangelist Joyce Carelock, Fairfax, VA; Mother, Judge Cassandra Louis, Chicago, IL; and Ms. Janice Bynum, Way Cross, GA, Lady Barbara Anderson, Charlotte, NC. Also, my cousin, Mother Mary McCarthy, attended two conferences from Kankakee IL., May God Bless you all!

My appreciation and sincere thanks to all for your loyalty and indescribable support. "The Many Apparels of Women Conference" was evident through all who exerted such efforts to win souls for Christ. Also, helped us identify ways to work together, in the outreach ministry for women of the church and communities.

TABLE OF CONTENTS

INTRODUCTION

I n the past God put me in positions to help
others, especially young women and families, through my professional career and my
church life. I have always loved mission work.
My desire is to educate women on who we are
on the inside, rather than the apparels we wear on
the outside. About 15 years ago, as the Assistant
State Supervisor, of the Alaska jurisdiction of the
Church of God in Christ Women's Department,
I wanted to do something that could benefit the
women I was selected to serve. During one of
our women's day programs, I began to pay close
attention to how the women conducted the service. Considering the thoughts of training, I began
to pray for direction, it came to me that women

wear many hats or do many jobs, and I began to think and work towards different approaches to train women working in the church.

My thought was to educate women in ministry, on how to face their various roles, pursue goals, and professional opportunities while becoming productive Christian women of today. I developed a strong desire to implement training opportunities, and activities to help women understand our inward purpose in the Kingdom of God. While I was focusing on the natural apparels of the women involved in the program that day, a thought came to me…as to how God has equipped women for the ministry of Christ. As women of God, we have love undisputable for our families and others. We have gifts and callings, undeniable knowledge, wisdom and understanding, that is often talent unsought for or unnoticed. As women, we are ready and capable of being used by God, in our homes, communities, on our jobs and certainly in the church.

My prayer was how could I inspire, motivate, and connect women together through the sharing of their inner abilities; while helping others grow. With a strong emphasis placed on encouraging women to use those treasures, they have on the inside to make the world a better place? After praying continually, I decided to make a plan for outreach. My thoughts focused on the many churches in the communities near, and abroad that could receive help through the training session.

There are many successful women in the world and we are also, and I said to myself, I can do this! At that point, I felt it was time to ask my leaders for permission to have a conference. The excitement began to rise in me; after much fasting and praying, my thoughts were made known unto my leaders. There is something about God's appointed time, which was evident. When discussing my vision with the State Supervisor; she immediately said, it sounds great. Keep in mind, this was the first conference, and at that time no plans were considered for future conferences. I thought this was a one-time event; my desire was to invite all the women's groups from the various churches within the communities.

By now my thoughts were in a whirl for a name of the conference, so the women would want to participate. During the next women's day service I attended the following month, I watched the participants with the beautiful suits, hats, and dresses; I became more aware of how much emphasis we place on the outfits we wear. We are more than pretty clothes and I love them too, but we are quality creatures with valuable assets to share with the world. After coming home and watching television, the first three commercials displayed were all women, with emphasis on their clothing, selling various goods, cereals for a family breakfast, autos for a large car dealer, and even properties. I exclaimed that's it! The Many Hats we wear that is my conference title! I focused on our various roles as mothers, home-makers, wives, nurses, doctors, lawyers, care-takers. Women are military members and spouses, city, federal, state and national workers; and Busy Church Ladies, to name a few.

However; in my spirit, I was yet unsettled about the title of the conference. There are many hats worn by women, and often we are misjudged by what we wear, our size, skin color, the church we attend etc., with much emphasis placed on how we look on the OUTSIDE. A thought came to me, Apparels! We have more to offer than apparels; we are more than that. I was constantly in prayer, seeking God's favor in choosing a title that was suitable to describe all that was in my heart. While attending a visiting church the following week, watching and listening to a young lady read the Scripture, afterward, she went back to her ushering duties wearing her black and white uniform. I received enlightenment, the conference name will be: *"THE MANY APPARELS OF WOMEN,"* THAT'S IT!

I envisioned a conference with workshops using presenters; and their personal stories to compare with the researched characters on topics about women in the Bible? Using the information shared as a guide to depict how God uses us in various ways, and for his purpose. I thought one creative way to get the women excited was to have a fashion show at the end of the program, for social interaction. We would have lunch while watching the fashions, and use models from all ages and stages of life, wearing beautiful age appropriate attire depicting Holy Women and their daughters. This marked the beginning of; The Many Apparels of Women's Conferences!

I stepped out in faith and implemented a plan to educate, motivate and rejuvenate women in the church to recognize their God given qualities through the conferences; and educate them on the various women's roles depicted in the Bible. My goal was to help women discover their inner beauty while increasing growth and enhancing their positions in the church.

The first conference held in 1999; it became very popular over the state of Alaska, and many other states. Ladies who had left Alaska came back and brought others to support my vision for the women. We had speakers from both far and near; and by the 10th year, the participants went from 53 to over 200. Participants came from 24 different churches and reformations by the tenth event. To God be the glory! After the first conference the ladies wanted to do it again and the next year more were in attendance and it continued to grow and be successful for ten consecutive years before it was ended, but my work was not over, The Lord yet had more for me to do. I have been busy with other trainings in different places in other states. Some ladies that participated in the conferences have gone on to begin other training and education events, so the work is still on-going.

As you read this book, I want you to have an overview and mental picture of each conference as it was presented. My prayer is that this book will be used as a self-help guide and motivator to direct women who are wearing many hats, and in need of guidance while discovering their hidden treasures and God's plan for their destiny.

BEAUTIFUL FROM THE INSIDE OUT

A woman that knows her self-worth, and the beauty from within, coupled with knowing her purpose in God is powerful beyond measure. The late Dr. Myles Munroe said, "Where purpose is not known, abuse is inevitable." As we strive to know ourselves; and prepare for life opportunities; let us also prepare for a spiritual awakening of our individual purposes. I must now ask you a question, is it possible that our created purpose is unknown, hence abused? God's Word helps us. "Wisdom is the principal thing; therefore get wisdom: and with all thy getting,

Get an understanding" (Proverbs 4:7). "Study to shew thyself approved unto God, a workman that needeth not to be ashamed, rightly dividing the word of truth" (2 Timothy 2:15). "My people are destroyed for lack of knowledge: because thou hast rejected Knowledge" (Hosea 4:6a).

Women we are misunderstood, and sometimes others focus more on the outer appearance than the inner beauty. You are valuable, never under sell yourself, and learn to walk away from opportunities that disgrace you as a person. When people gawk at you, recognize that they might see a body used for pleasure, and then soon forgotten. God sees a Queen that is priceless, and wants to use her to build His Kingdom.

We are recognized from secular perspectives as advertisement, our bodies are constantly sexualized and objectified, and even eye-candy to bring notoriety to others. On the other hand, sometimes women are devalued based on past challenges, and the pitfalls of life. Regardless of your story.

A woman who had children out of wedlock, being in an inappropriate relationship, or you are suffering from an identity crises; God has a plan and purpose for your life. Stop focusing on public opinion, and start focusing on the beauty inside of you.

My prayer is that as godly women, we show godly characteristics during life's challenges. We need to know who we are, our capabilities, and the necessity of looking on the inside for the beauty within; although, we agree that clothing is important and people judge us inevitably sometimes by what we wear. Let me introduce to you the body armor that is necessary to help apparel fit better. One might think, "Lingerie" how can it help me recognize the beauty on the inside.

Let's look at the Scripture and see the importance of body armor (godly lingerie), as our protection "Stand therefore, having your loins girt about with truth, and having on the breastplate of righteousness. (Ephesian 6:14).

"Put on the whole armour of God
that ye may be able to stand against

the wiles of the devil. For we wrestle not against flesh and blood, but against principalities, against powers, against the rulers of the darkness of this world, against spiritual wickedness in high places."

Ephesians 6:11-12

Women have many roles, and it is important to know who we are inside. Across the globe, working woman encounter challenges including failed relationships, which reflect their performance at home, work, and church. Although, it is important to discuss who we are, we should understand our role as helpers, God created *Eve*, she was a help for Adam. Women have been in many situations to aid and assist men on many levels. As we look at the many women in the Bible, which one of the women might represent a portion of you on the inside? Women are mothers, sisters, doctors, lawyers, etc.; all of the things the world need. Also, women are firewomen, police officers, and bankers. Let us realize that we have a purpose, and God made women giving us a role in society and the church. We have a role in the Kingdom of God that determines our destiny. Let us not forget our modest apparel and the many "hats" we wear. Remember as the Word says:

> "Whose adorning let it not be that outward adorning of plaiting the hair, and of wearing of gold, or of putting on of apparel; 4 but let it be the hidden man of the heart, in that which is not corruptible, even the ornament of a meek and quiet spirit, which is in the sight of God of great price."
>
> 1 Peter 3:3-4

We can be "saved, and look good," first from the inside followed by the outward appearance. In the Scripture, *Queen Esther* was in the palace to help the Jews. She took on the role of a leader;

it was Esther who called the people to prayer and fasting. Women there are many things we can do, and will do when called upon for the sake of God's people. It is important to know who we are, what we can do, and how to administer help to others.

When we recognize who we are on the inside; and the importance of godly apparel, our witness and testimony is most effective. There are others in the Bible that were used to cultivate and help shape godly women characters. Women are mentors, women of hospitality, leaders, and they are all in the family of God. *Esther* shows us how to wait on God, and embrace those life challenges recognizing that God is able, and he will take you through your various encounters. Look at the Scriptures, as *Esther* bade them return Mordecai this answer:

> "Go, gather together all the Jews that
> are present in Shushan, and fast ye
> for me, and neither eat nor drink

three days, night or day: I also and
my maidens will fast likewise; and
so will I go in unto the king, which
is not according to the law: and if I
perish , I perish."

Esther 4:16-17

Let's look at *Priscilla and Aquila*; Priscilla
took an active role in support of her husband in
the ministry. They opened their home as a place
of worship and became followers of Christ and
workers with Paul as he ministered throughout
Asia. "The churches of Asia salute you. *Aquila
and Priscilla* salute you much in the Lord, with
the church that is in their house" (1 Corinthians
16:19). As women, we can feel overwhelmed at
times, being there for the home and the family.
We must realize that the beginning of a complete
society starts in the home. Women in ministry
must also be capable of balancing home, work,
and church life. We must be able to show the love
and ministry of Christ in our lives at all times.

"Who can find a virtuous woman? For her price is far above rubies" (Proverbs 31:10).

We are vulnerable to many relationships that are not always easy; for example, a leadership role as a woman. When we get into areas where we may be called leaders, it is important that we are subject to God's will and guidance to maintain positive relationships. Sometimes the roles of women are misunderstood. The many hats that women wear can be various and simultaneous; such as a working woman, community leader, church supporter as well as a homemaker. In the corporate world, it is called task management; however, women have always been capable of multi-tasking in their managing abilities. As nurturers, helpers, and teachers, we balance multiple roles on a daily basis. Thus, we embrace *"The Many Apparels of Women."*

Women we must have confidence in ourselves knowing that God has placed value in each of us. It is not what others say about us, but what we say to ourselves. Your outside beauty is not a reflection of your inside value. Many have made costly mistakes looking on the outside instead of seeing the treasures on the inside. "I will praise you; for I am fearfully and wonderfully made: marvelous are your works; and that my soul knows right well" (Psalm 139:14). We can model the outward apparel because the inside is in control. We are fearfully and wonderfully made and appareled by God.

HER NAME IS WOMAN

S ome women have the characteristics of a godly woman and do many things that represent God in a positive light. Let's explore the lives of several women as our examples, who are mothers, grandmothers, and leaders in the Bible. Deborah was a leader in Israelites; she solved their disagreements. The Bible calls her a prophetess, or woman prophet. Deborah encouraged Barak to trust God. She did not want to usurp authority over him; so instead, she encouraged him to do the things that God called him to do. She expressed these powerful words to him, "I will go with you, and I will work with you" (Judges 4:9). Deborah understood her role and purpose; and not once did she attempt to exercise authority over Barak, the leader at the time; however, she was essential in getting the job done.

Leah, *Huldah*, and *Anna* are great biblical examples. "*Her name is Woman*," she appears to each of us distinctively and perhaps in different manners. She may not be known by name, her actions, or her outside apparel, but she knows her purpose and on the inside she is in control. We must be obedient to God in all that we do. God has a plan for each of us, and he supplies our needs, desires, and the things of purpose. "The angel of the Lord encampeth round about them that fear him, and delivereth them" (Psalm 37:4).

Job's wife—we may not know her name, however, we know she was a woman chosen by God. You may be a plain woman, but God can beautify you. "For the LORD taketh pleasure in his people: he will beautify the meek with salvation" (Psalm 149:4). God will make you the woman He would have you to be. We do not all look the same or act the same; however, we all have a purpose given to us by God. We do not have to justify our being, but we should be content in the woman God have called us to become. Many of us believe the hardships endured by Job, was also felt by his wife. She watched her children die while her husband suffered from his illnesses.

"And there was a day when his sons and his daughters were eating and drinking wine in their eldest brother's house: And there came a messenger unto Job, and said, the oxen were plowing, and the asses feeding beside them: And the Sabeans fell upon them and took them away; yea, they have slain the servants with the edge of the sword; and I only am escaped alone to tell thee. While he was yet speaking, there came also another, and said, the fire of God is fallen from heaven, and hath burned up the sheep, and the servants, and consumed them, and I only am escaped alone to tell thee."

Job 1:13-19

We may never understand how Job's wife felt, ten times God had blessed her womb; and he allowed her to love, nurture, and raise her children in the fear of God; and now she experiences great loss. Job's wife was no doubt influential in her family's life. Can you imagine the grief that overwhelmed her soul as she looked down in disbelief as they buried her ten children? She experienced the loss of all her children, financial loss, and her husband suffered sickness with physical disfigurement. In light of what she had gone through, we can identify with her story and her pain. She is known by the coined phrase, "curse God and die." Perhaps she was at a low place in life, that to her it was better for her husband to end it all by disrespecting God. She was not focusing on the blessings that would come after, and I am sure her faith at that point had become stagnate as she watched the downfall of her family. *My personal testimony, of being a caretaker for a sick husband for ten years, I can understand her pain, how about you?*

Leah and Rachel were sisters; Jacob arranged with their father to marry Rachel. Instead, Jacob was tricked by Laban, and given Leah the older daughter; which was the custom during that time. Jacob was willing to work another seven years for Rachel. Leah was plain, and Rachel was beautiful. We must remember the Scripture:

> "But the LORD said unto Samuel, Look not on his countenance, or on the height of his stature; because I have refused him: for the LORD seeth not as man seeth; for man looketh on the outward appearance, but the LORD looketh on the heart."
>
> 1Samuel 16:7

For those of you who are seeking God for a mate, he will make you the perfect helper for the desired husband if you trust God to direct your life. Let's image how Leah felt, given to a man who wanted someone else. I am sure many of us can identify with Leah; a woman who was rejected, and we know from the Scriptures that Jacob didn't love her. Although he loved Rachel, he nevertheless treated Leah as if she was payment for services rendered. "And Jacob said unto Laban, Give me my wife, for my days are fulfilled, that I may go in unto her" (Genesis 29:21). I am sure these two women felt as if life was squeezed out of them. Regardless of what you might be going through right now, I want to encourage you, my sisters that The Lord will vindicate you. Let's focus on the Word of God:

> "Now the LORD saw that Leah was unloved, and He opened her womb, but Rachel was barren. Leah conceived and bore a son and named

him Reuben, for she said, "Because the LORD has seen my affliction; surely now my husband will love me." Then she conceived again and bore a son and said, "Because the LORD has heard that I am unloved, He has therefore given me this son also." So she named him Simeon. She conceived again and bore a son and said, "Now this time my husband will become attached to me, because I have borne him three sons." Therefore he was named Levi. And she conceived again and bore a son and said, "This time I will praise the LORD." Therefore she named him Judah. Then she stopped bearing."

Genesis 29:31-35

Although Leah, was not beautiful in the sight of man, she yet had the favor of God. Leah was not forgotten—God knew her name! The Scriptures emphatically displays God's love and faithfulness for His children." In the verses below we are able to see God's dialogue between the *Children of Israel*. Look at the rejection in their speech to God, "The LORD has abandoned us…forgotten us." Look at how God compares His love for Zion as the love of a mother for her child. The Lord assures Zion that he is not like mothers by saying, "Even these mothers may forget…I will not forget you! Look at God's passion and love shown to His people, and the Scriptures holds true today as well.

> "But Zion said, "The LORD has forsaken me, the Lord has forgotten me." "Can a mother forget the baby at her breast and have no compassion on the child she has borne? Though she may forget, I will not forget you! See, I have engraved you on the palms of my hands; your walls are ever before me. Can a

mother forget the baby at her breast and have no compassion on the child she has borne? Though she may forget, I will not forget you!"

Isaiah 49:14-16 NIV

Sisters' are you dealing with some painful circumstances today and think God has forgotten about you? Maybe you think He's abandoned you and doesn't care what you are going through. Do you sometimes feel deserted, or forsaken, left behind and unwanted? Let me assure you through God's Word. Although people may abandon us, people we love and have a life history with, God will *never* abandon us. Rest assured my sisters **God Knows Your Name!** As women of God, we must understand, God is in charge. He has a plan and purpose for us, and will give us what He desires us to have. Wear the apparels God has given you and be faithful.

Huldah was another ordinary woman that God used to do extraordinary things. She was an example of many women serving the Lord in ministry. She was an approved prophetess of the Lord, and was consulted by Josiah, the penitent king of Judah. She sent him such a thrilling message from the Lord that caused all Judah and Jerusalem to tremble and turn to the Lord." We can be used by God in the same way, if we allow Him.

> "And Hilkiah, and they that the king had appointed, went to Huldah the prophetess, the wife of Shallum the son of Tikvath, the son of Hasrah, keeper of the wardrobe; (now she dwelt in Jerusalem in the college:) and they spake to her to that effect. And she answered them, Thus saith the LORD God of Israel, Tell ye the man that sent you to me, Thus saith the LORD, … Because thine heart was tender, and thou didst humble thyself before God, when thou

heardest his words against this place, and against the inhabitants thereof, and humbledst thyself before me, and didst rend thy clothes, and weep before me; I have even heard thee also, saith the LORD."

2 Chronicles 34:22-27

Anna a prophetess and a mature worshipper of God; women maturity gives you the stamina needed to hold on in difficult times. After the death of her husband, perhaps she could have remarried, but she chose to share her faith to as many people as she could. She chose to serve the Lord, fast and pray, and to worship the Lord day and night. Anna chose to tell others about the Savior that was coming, no matter how long it might be before he came. She knew her purpose and she did not allow the opinions of others to deter her from it. Anna's choice to worship not only affected her life, but also the lives of women today.

We need to be more assured of ourselves, and share our testimonies, to help others. The purpose of many types of apparel of women is to help women of all stages of life to work together understanding what we can offer to help others. Concentrate on yourself and your talents, who you are, and what you can share with others.

A prayer warrior who is a banker or a corporate CEO, a nurse, or a grandma caring for her grandchildren, those traits of compassion, and love are evident in women of destiny. You are where you are for a reason, let's strive to make the best of it. It's your contribution to those around you, consider it your ministry for someone to observe.

What valuable treasures do you have on the inside that can help the ministry, the Pastor, and other outreach workers? Take the challenge, and help others shine and gracefully deal with your female encounters, it's a part of life, not necessarily a problem. "Your name is Woman," encompasses much thought to provoke questions, and to lets us know we are on a mission with God's help we can do it. "I can do all this through him who gives me strength" (Phil 4:13).

Perhaps, their stories affects each of us in a different manner. God has a plan for each of us. He supplies our needs, and the tools needed for women to be in control of life's situations.

AGES AND STAGES, A WOMAN'S LIFE'S JOURNEY

The ages and stages of a woman's life's journey determines her *created being* at any time. We can apply this to both youth and the most mature ladies of wisdom. It is good for both the young and an older woman to grow together in God. Let's look at the ages and stages of life, and how it benefits younger women and older women as well in knowing our place in the Kingdom of God.

Consider the life passages of the biblical women spoken of in the Scriptures. Let us seek to recognize our stages in life and to use the biblical information shared to make better choices as we continue our life's journey. In the Bible days, there were many challenges experienced by a woman, and so it is today. Older ladies know a lot that you may not have experienced yet, don't disregard their knowledge and wisdom. Consider them useful, they were once your age, and might be able to help you cope with life's challenges.

Dinah: The daughter of Jacob and Leah, an innocent victim, like many women today who have been victimized because of curiosity causing her to make poor choices, and maybe not having reputable or qualified mentors. She grew curious enough to leave the safety of the camp and to go see what was going on; and she drew attention from men, and girls of that time. Her trip into town was unwise, she went out of her family's camp, left its safety, specifically to see the "daughters of the land."

> "And Dinah the daughter of Leah, which she bare unto Jacob, went out to see the daughters of the land. And when Shechem the son of Hamor

the Hivite, prince of the country, saw her, he took her, and lay with her, and defiled her."

Genesis 34:1-2

Jochebed provided nourishment for her children, cared for her family and was practical.

Sometimes we give our children too much, and we forget the important principles of respect, morals and values taught to us as children. Many of us feel that our children should not want for anything, but at what expense have we created a generation that has a sense of entitlement? Jochebed shows us how through wisdom, and creativity, she was able to save the life of her son Moses from the destruction of slaughter of baby boys, which was pronounced by Pharaoh. We must save our children from the enemy, and be accountable to God. Whatever God wants you to do, be obedient to Him.

"And there went a man of the house of Levi, and took to wife a daughter of Levi. And the woman conceived, and bare a son: and when she saw him that he was a goodly child, she hid him three months. And when she could no longer hide him, she took for him an ark of bulrushes, and daubed it with slime and with pitch, and put the child therein; and she laid it in the flags by the river's brink. And his sister stood afar off, to wit what would be done to him. And the daughter of Pharaoh came down to wash herself at the river, and her maidens walked along by the river's side; and when she saw the ark among the flags, she sent her maid to fetch it. And when she had opened it, she saw the child: and, behold, the babe wept. And she had compassion on him, and said, this is one of the Hebrews' children. Then said his sister to Pharaoh's daughter, Shall I go and call to thee a nurse of the Hebrew women, that she may nurse the child for thee? And Pharaoh's daughter said to her, Go. And the maid went and called the child's mother. And Pharaoh's daughter said unto her, Take this child away, and nurse it for me, and I will give thee thy wages. And the women took the child and nursed it. And the child grew, and she brought him unto Pharaoh's daughter, and he became her son. And she called his name Moses: and she said because I drew him out of the water."

Exodus 2:1-10

Lydia, a Christ-honoring woman, was an example of a hardworking business professional. God has an expectation for us all, and it is time for a change. "She worshipped God," we are told. Often business people are engrossed in their affairs and do not have time for God. But Lydia, in spite of all her secular obligations, found time to worship God. She knew that in order to successfully meet the stiff competition of the Philippian traders, she needed grace as well as knowledge.

You may be blessed to have a successful career, or own your own business, if so, manage with perfection; *Lydia* was a mentor with a successful business; and she did things with the spirit of excellence. Church ladies we are needed for the families, communities, and our churches as mentors, and educators so that those coming after us will have examples.

> "A certain woman named Lydia, a seller of purple, of the city of Thyatira, which worshipped God, heard us: whose heart the Lord opened, that she attended unto the things which were spoken of Paul.

And when she was baptized, and her household, she besought us, saying, if ye have judged me to be faithful to the Lord, come into my house, and abide there. And she constrained us."

Acts 16:15-15

God has a plan for all ages and stages of life. Women, we can be professional women that honors Christ, seek God in all our endeavors. The Scripture encourages us to share what we have with others and we shall be blessed:

"And we beseech you, brethren, to know them which labour among you, and are over you in the Lord, and admonish you; And to esteem them very highly in love for their work's sake. And be at peace among yourselves."

1 Thessalonica 5:12-13

Lydia was not a person of just living for the now; she used Purple in her business that was very expensive, and she wanted the best. We should strive for the spirit of excellence in all that we do, and seek God for direction. Her products were not cheap, and yet she was willing to share and displayed great hospitality. When God blesses you don't forget where you came from, use wisdom and consider others. Let us be woman of worth and godly standards!

Being in the right place, doing the right thing, at the right time is usually not a coincident. It is a part of your chosen purpose in life. Young women, be observant of those around you, seek mentorship. As we mature, pass on the knowledge, you have learned and bless others.

"The aged women likewise, that they be in behaviour as becometh holiness, not false accusers, not given to much wine, teachers of good things; That they may teach the young women to be sober, to love their husbands, to love their children, To be discreet, chaste, keepers at home, good, obedient to their own husbands, that the word of God be not blasphemed."

Titus 2:3-5

You can be anything you want to be, if we have the potential to be a leader, do it with all your heart, mind and soul. If you are in the *following-stage*, do it faithfully, and with diligence. We can wear professional hats along with being the CEO of motherhood, or any other venture you decide. We must seek God for the hat that fits us, NOT the one for someone else. There are many of you destined for greatness, seek God for yourself and you will receive the benefits.

Also, in relationships, we wear many hats, and we are multi-taskers at all times. Our characters are models, and on the outside a reflection of your inner characteristics in your daily presentations. What stage of your life are you experiencing?

WOMEN STANDING WITH INTEGRITY AND CONFIDENCE IN ADVERSE SITUATIONS

As women, some adversities come from being subject to others. Many times, we are misunderstood and maybe not considered at all; however, we must seek God. May your soul say, "Yes" as God leads you, walk and know that you are called to stand on the promises of his Word. In this chapter, three biblical women identified as expressing confidence along with their integrity. "Judge me, oh Lord; for I have walked in mine integrity; I have also trusted in the Lord; therefore, I shall not slide" (Psalm 26:1). The women are *Deborah,* who let Barak know she had his back. Deborah, whose bravery saved not only her life but also the lives of her people? She knew her place and never tried to overstep her bounds. She was a professional woman who was beneficial. You can do this too, if called upon.

> "And Deborah, a prophetess, the wife of Lapidoth, she judged Israel at that time. And she dwelt under the palm tree of Deborah between Ramah and Bethel in mount Ephraim: and the children of Israel came up to her for judgment. And she sent and called Barak the son of Abinoam out of Kedeshnaphtali, and said unto him, Hath not the LORD God of Israel commanded, saying, Go and draw toward mount Tabor, and take with thee ten thousand men of the children of Naphtali and of the children of Zebulun? And I will draw

unto thee to the river Kishon Sisera, the captain of Jabin's army, with his chariots and his multitude; and I will deliver him into thine hand. And Barak said unto her, If thou wilt goes with me, then I will go: but if thou wilt not go with me, then I will not go. And she said I will surely go with thee: notwithstanding the journey that thou takest shall not be for thine honour; for the LORD shall sell Sisera into the hand of a woman. And Deborah arose, and went with Barak to Kedesh."

Judges 4:4-9; 5:1-3

Mary, the mother of Jesus, willing in such adverse situations to say to the Lord with dignity, "My soul says yes, and her life went from agony to glory when she knew she had borne a Savior for the world.

"To a virgin espoused to a man whose name was Joseph, of the house of David; and the virgin's name was Mary. And the angel came in unto her, and said, Hail, thou that art highly favoured, the Lord is with thee: blessed art thou among women. And when she saw him, she was troubled at his saying and cast in her mind what manner of salutation this should be. And the angel said unto her, Fear not, Mary: for thou hast found favour with God. And, behold, thou shalt conceive in thy womb, and bring forth a son, and shalt call his name JESUS."

Luke 1:27-31

Deborah was a woman of culture, a woman of grace and a woman that knows her place in the Lord. Sometimes we have to take a strong stand with integrity. All God needs from us is to say yes Lord; I am willing. Today Integrity seems very weak among many, but we must stand strong because our roles are much more important than before. Many single mothers are heads of the household, which could be an adverse situation.

Sometimes we must do as *Esther* did, put on royal apparel, look good, and pray. Also, ask God for Wisdom and speak up; by doing so you could help save the family members or someone in the community, or in the church. Also, SAVE yourself, your job both natural and spiritual. Be it known, that sometimes "man" will threaten to take it from you, but God has not given you a spirit of fear because you are a woman of many apparels. You are chosen by God, and you are one of his children of purpose; know that he has given you power.

Speaking of adversity, *Esther* was also a very courageous and steadfast woman. She appeared to have been taught to pray, and how to deal with a crisis. *Esther* humbled herself, even though she was considered beautiful with wisdom and social graces there was a special service in God's plan for her life and the Jews. She was appareled and had physical access to the King that others didn't have. Also, her cousin Mordecai, who raised her, knew her outer beauty would cause the King to select her into the palace. It was evident that Mordecai taught her wisdom, respect and honor for God with great faith.

> "For if thou altogether holdest thy peace at this time, then shall there enlargement and deliverance arise to the Jews from another place; but thou and thy father's house shall be destroyed: and who knoweth whether thou art comes to the kingdom for such a time as this? Then Esther bade them return Mordecai this answer, go gather together all the Jews that are present in Shushan, and fast ye for me, and neither eat nor drink three days, night or day: I

also and my maidens will fast likewise; and so will I go in unto the king, which is not according to the law: and if I perish, I perish."

Esther 4:14-16

You may on occasions feel betrayed by a friend, or a mate with unexpected disappointment. Don't allow your family to be placed in jeopardy. However, keep the confidence and your integrity, it could give you joy, peace and happiness, your inward control can save a marriage and your family or more. Esther saved her life and the lives of her nation who gained relief from their enemies; and she remained the wife of the King.

Mary said yes to the Lord, in a very challenging situation, she had her integrity that gave her prime confidence. Deborah and Esther were empowered by God. Esther was willing to die for the love of her people. Love will give you courage and confidence in any situation as women maintain your Integrity. "And the second is like, namely this, Thou shalt love thy neighbour as thyself. There is none another commandment greater than these" (Mark 12:31).

WOMEN OF GOD WALKING AND WORKING IN WISDOM

This chapter gives us the opportunity to start where we are with the woman within us to accomplish more for God in our homes. Wisdom must be a priority to maintain togetherness and family unity; spouse's needs and want to be respected. We are in lead positions to see this happen with husbands, children, relatives such as in-laws and even our distant family members; and community, schools, on the jobs and especially in our neighborhoods.

Take a look at yourself and ask, what you would do, or have done if you were Abigail.

Remembering Genesis 1: 18, we were made as help meets to spouses; mothers, trainers, guides and examples in our homes and to all we encounter. God will give us the knowledge and the wisdom to do things successfully well if we allow Him.

Abigail was caught in a situation that called for her to use her strength. She stepped up and made a decision to do a job that her husband should have accomplished, but had allowed himself to Become unable, so she went out and got the job done as the king requested and the situation was taken care of with her use of wisdom. In our decisions, we must be wise; and let your good works speak for you. Working together means living to reach others and keeping open communication, actions and support for all those we have daily contact or occasional personal interactions.

Ruth was a prime example of a woman of good character and respect for others, especially her mother in law Naomi. She was obedient and was blessed with another husband after her husband died. As we look at Ruth's story, take a look and see if we measure up to what is required of us. Ruth was Wisdom Personified.

Dorcas, A woman full of good works; and Abigail, a woman, determined to walk in wisdom to represent the man she married. Sometimes we must realize that some things are family matters, and you just have to get the job done. Be the helper at the time of need. "My people are destroyed for the lack of knowledge: because thou hast rejected knowledge (Hosea 4:6a).   "Wisdom is the principal thing; therefore get wisdom: and with the getting get understanding" (Proverbs 4:7).

As we study the story of the life of Ruth, Dorcas, and Abigail. Let's take a look at ourselves. Are you displaying love, caring and sharing with wisdom for others? We must examine our actions and see if we meet God's standards. Who are we portraying and who did God make us to be. Ask yourself, am I that person? What are my goals, and am I making the sufficient efforts to accomplish them? Learn to seek wisdom, so that as we work together we walk in peace, as we are capable of doing.

Dorcas classified as a disciple in her time for her good works. She belonged to one of the earliest Christians congregations. She was known for her practical works of mercy. Her joy was to serve Jesus by serving those in need. Give and God will give it back to you, don't be selfish or greedy; continue to Walk and Work in wisdom.

ADORNED AND SUITABLY FIT FOR KINGDOM WORK

We elaborated on being dressed and fit strong enough for Kingdom work at any age. *Sara* the wife of Abraham for many years she had no children, and the Lord said she would conceive in her old age. Sarah did not understand bearing a son, so she sent her maid to conceive a child when Abraham was 86 years old. When she was over 90-years-old, God gave her a child and blessed them to become the head of a nation. What God has for you it is for you! We must trust, believe and rely on God; Sarah did, and it happened. We must apparel ourselves for the mission that God has for us because he prepares us for our destiny, but we must believe. Sarah became an intricate part of the human race. Women today more than 2000 years later; may be called to do things differently, and beyond the norm. If God says it, that settles it! There is nothing too hard for God.

Pricilla, a leading Evangelist of the early church, she was a woman understanding faith and helped to build the church. She experienced opposition for sharing the gospel, from both Jews and Gentiles; however, she was suitably dressed for the occasion. Her joy was to spread the gospel and nurture the church. Priscilla and husband Aquilla met Paul, she had been planted in an atmosphere of strife and controversy in Rome and later in Corinth. They were in a wealthy seaport, not the ideal place to nurture and bring forth new believers, but God transplanted them there, and that is where they went. Paul, a Jew was a persecutor of Jesus and his followers. They met in the community both tent makers. They invited Paul in to stay with them, and he stayed 18-months, and they all left together to further the ministry when Paul left Ephesus. Priscilla and her husband were changed. She became a spiritually mature woman whose gifts equipped her for leadership. Her name Precedes Acquilla in several scriptures mentioned in the New Testament.

> "Who shall separate us from the love of Christ? Shall tribulation, or distress, or persecution, or famine, or nakedness, or peril, or sword? As it is written, for thy sake we are killed all the day long; we are accounted as sheep for the slaughter. Nay, in all these things we are more than conquerors through him that loved us. For I am persuaded, that neither death, nor life, nor angels, nor principalities, nor powers, nor things present, nor things to come, nor height, nor depth, nor any other creature, shall be able to separate

us from the love of God, which is
in Christ Jesus our Lord."

Rom 8:35, 37-39

We have spiritual mature middle age women
that can contribute to ministry. Think about where
you are and what you can offer to others, and to
the ministry. Be a help to your pastor and the
pastors wife, elderly and the children. Remember
you are clothed and beautiful from the inside out.
Ladies if you have a gift there is a great opportunity for you to step out on your faith, and do
God's will.

Do not settle for the status quo, despite your
surroundings. Let God use you, to get His work
done by supporting your husband and or others.
God will bring out the leadership qualities, and
your gifts will make room for you. Wait on the
Lord and do not be discouraged if things don't
come right away. God's timing is not our timing,
and His ways are not our ways. He will fulfill His
purpose for you. "Wait on the Lord: be of good

courage, and he shall strengthen thine heart: wait, I say, on the Lord" (Psalm 27:14).

The *Samaritan woman* was looked down upon in the neighborhood while she was a chosen vessel for Christ to send out as a witness as to who he was. They were waiting for the Messiah, when she met Jesus at the well. Jesus told her about the water of life, and he told her of her past and present way of living. Little did the community know she would be the one to witness to them About Christ? Our outer apparel does not tell what's on the inside, the purpose God has for us or our destinies. The Woman at the well had her sins washed away by Jesus Divine Mercy. He will do the same for you and me. The woman did not know Jesus, but he told her he was the Messiah, the Christ she awaited. She repented of her sins and went out to tell family and friends, and many wanted to go and see Him. St. John 4:16-18 she went on to lead many to conversion through her zeal and love for God.

When we meet and become acquainted with the Lord and give our lives to Him, we will have a living testimony to share drawing men to God. This woman was fitted for Kingdom work after she met Jesus. It is wise to be aware of the difference in Kingdom work and Church work. This woman may not have been a typical church working person yet, but she had a message for the world about Jesus, one that will help others receive eternal life. We must adorn ourselves with the whole armor of God for Kingdom work.

GODLY WOMEN SOARING IN MINISTRY BEYOND EXPECTATION

I n this chapter, we are focusing on Women expounding in the ministry. A Scripture I was led to during a personal incident, was the *daughters of Zelophahad*, these daughters put forth an effort to see that justice was done and got an answer from God through His servant Moses. "Why should the name of our father be done away from among his family, because he hath no son? Give unto us therefore a possession among the brethren of our father" (Numbers 27:4). They stood their grounds. Our Focus: *"Receive your portion."*

Women don't be so easy to give up on what God has given you, because it is not expected of you. We all have a right to excel anywhere, and anytime God gives us something to share, we must be willing to share your portion with ordinary people. When the daughters of Zelophehad realized, after their father died, that the laws of the day would give his properties to outsiders rather than to the five sisters. Those sisters felt they deserved their portion of the inheritance. They soared beyond expectation and took their case to their leaders.

Today it would need to be a change of laws to grant equality, but Moses brought their case before the Lord, and the Lord said the daughters are right, and they were granted their portion. The ruling brought hope to the Israelites that the daughters have the same rights as sons. "Yea, the Lord will answer and say unto his people, Behold, I will send you corn, and wine, and oil, and ye shall be satisfied therewith: and I will no more make you a reproach among the heathen.

The Law was changed" (Joel 2:19). We can rest assured the Lord will rightfully provide for His people both male and female.

We are one in Christ, and we have a mission for Him. Today we have Many Apparels of Women being displayed. We the women are beginning to soar in the gifts, talents and the, knowledge of God by spreading the gospel to all with wisdom; in our homes, communities, networking through the media and more. Our communication with God and the sacrifice of obedience has drawn nations to hope and salvation. Our ministries are stronger than ever before and to many, Beyond mans' Expectations, but the word says, "There is neither male nor female in Christ" (Galatians 3:28). We are one body; let us claim, receive and display your portions of the ministry. Where ever and whenever possible.

Recognize and explore your ministries, by sharing your, position with ordinary people. God uses ordinary people to do extra-ordinary things. An ordinary woman, who met Jesus at the well, was picked out and chosen by Him to go and take the world a message of life from Him. She was able to minister, to the ordinary people in her circle of friends and with the ordinary folk of the neighborhood. She was able to use her story as a witness. She told them to come and see a man that told me everything that I had done. She raised their curiosity about the Messiah and the people came and followed her. She soared beyond the expectation of all those she reached with her testimony.

Those of us who have a relationship with God are truly qualified to do the same as the woman at the well. She was chosen and sent there to meet Jesus and receive that message for the people. If you are chosen of God, He qualifies you to do the same. Many times, we have stronger messages because of our personal experiences. We are able to invite, recruit and impart our ministry through witnessing. We are ready and capable to live, display and relay to the world our knowledge of the goodness of the Lord. When we provide messages to those around us, even if they think WOW! I did not expect that from a Woman, just know, if God has anointed you to reach out to the world, it may be far beyond their Expectations, but not of Gods.' You are also bought with a price, a peculiar people and a chosen vessel of the Lord to Soar in His Ministry. Now is the time to exercise the callings upon your life. Continue in your Ministries moving forward following the example of the Holy Scriptures. You are free to act on your calling.

> "For as many of you as have been baptized into Christ have put on Christ. There is neither Jew nor Greek, there is neither bond nor free, there is neither male nor female: for ye are all one in Christ Jesus. And if ye be Christ's, then are ye Abraham's seed, and heirs according to the promise."
>
> Gal 3:26-29

TAKING AUTHORITY THROUGH CHRIST IN PURSUIT OF MY DESTINY

We have the authority of God through Christ to reach our aims, goals, objectives, and to reach an expected end of prosperity with successful results. When women explore their destiny, it is a stage of independency of mind, body and soul. We are created from man's body, and became his help meet with authority through Christ to reach our aims, goals, objectives, and to reach an expected end of prosperity and good results. The Scriptures verify our existence:

"And the LORD God said, it is not good that the man should be alone; I will make him a help meet for him. And out of the ground the LORD God formed every beast of the field, and every fowl of the air; and brought them unto Adam to see what he would call them: and whatsoever Adam called every living creature that was the name thereof. And Adam gave names to all cattle, and to the fowl of the air, and to every beast of the field; but for Adam there was not found a help meet for him. And the LORD God caused a deep sleep to fall upon Adam, and he slept: and he took one of his ribs, and closed up the flesh instead thereof; And the rib, which the LORD God had taken from man, made he a woman, and brought her unto the man."

Gen 2:18-22

There is never a need to doubt having the ability to yearn for a glorious destiny. One's destiny determines their strengths pursuit. Women are strong beings and must keep many goals in mind as we learn and delve into our futures. We must have an endeavor to strive in spite of the negative elements of the world around us; Christ gives us the strength needed to survive. Many women of the Bible days were powerful leaders and their names were never mentioned; however, their apparel of commitment was evident in many ways. Some examples are: *Job's wife*, the *woman at the well*, the S*hunammite woman*, and even the *real mother of the illegitimate child* who said, let the child live and the King awarded her the baby because of her love for the child. Then came two women that were harlots, unto the king, and stood before him. The King delivered the child to his mother, it pays to be honest because God knows your heart.

"And the one woman said, O my lord, I and this woman dwell in one house; and I was delivered of a child with her in the house. And it came to pass the third day after that I was delivered, that this woman was delivered also: and we were together; there was no stranger with us in the house, save we two in the house. And this woman's child died in the night; because she overlaid it. And she arose at midnight, and took my son from beside me, while thine handmaid slept, and laid it in her bosom, and laid her dead child in my bosom. And when I rose in the morning to give my child suck, behold, it was dead: but when I had considered it in the morning, behold, it was not my son, which I did bear. And the other woman said, nay; but the living is my son, and the dead is thy son. And this said, No; but the dead is thy son, and the living is my son. Thus they spake before the king. Then said the king, the one saith, this is my son that liveth, and thy son is the dead: and the other saith, nay; but thy son is the dead, and my son is the living. And the king said, Bring me a sword. And they brought a sword before the king. And the king said, Divide the living child in two, and give half to the one, and half to the other. Then spake the woman who's the living child was unto the king, for her bowels yearned upon her son, and she said, O my lord, give her the living child, and in no wise slay it. But the other said, Let it be neither mine nor thine, but divide it."

1 Kings 3:16-26

The *Shunamite* woman was apparel with love, kindness, and patience, she was clever and respectful. Her efforts of hospitality made her family a success. Our goals today should be to reach out with faith and hope that will add to us, as well as to demonstrate our pursuit toward destiny. She was one whom hospitality led her to give aid to the prophet, and she gracefully used the proper approach to work with her husband on the decisions that needed to be made.

> "And it fell on a day, that Elisha passed to Shunem, where was a great woman; and she constrained him to eat bread. And so it was, that as oft as he passed by, he turned in thither to eat bread. And she said unto her husband, Behold now, I perceive that this is a holy man of God, which passeth by us continually. Let us make a little chamber, I pray thee, on the wall; and let us

set for him there a bed, and a table, and a stool, and a candlestick: and it shall be, when he cometh to us that he shall turn in thither. And it fell on a day, that he came thither, and he turned into the chamber, and lay there. And he said to Gehazi his servant, Call this Shunammite. And when he had called her, she stood before him. And he said unto him, Say now unto her, Behold, thou hast been careful for us with all this care; what is to be done for thee? Wouldest thou be spoken for to the king, or to the captain of the host? And she answered, I dwell among mine own people. And he said, what then is to be done for her? And Gehazi answered, verily she hath no child, and her husband is old. And he said, call her. And when he had called her, she stood in the door. And he

said, about this season, according to
the time of life, thou shalt embrace
a son. And she said, Nay, my lord,
thou man of God, do not lie unto
thine handmaid."

2 Kings 4:8-17

The *Queen of Sheba* knew her powers, and limits could control her destiny. She sought wisdom over her natural power. She was fascinated over the rumors of Solomon's Wisdom and riches. She travelled from afar to Jerusalem to see for herself the profound Wisdom of Solomon. What she heard from the king's lips and saw of his wealth and power astounded her.

"And when the queen of Sheba heard
of the fame of Solomon concerning
the name of the LORD, she came to
prove him with hard questions. And
she came to Jerusalem with a very
great train, with camels that bare

spices, and very much gold, and precious stones: and when she was come to Solomon, she communed with him of all that was in her heart. And Solomon told her all her questions: there was not anything hid from the king, which he told her not. And when the queen of Sheba had seen all Solomon's wisdom, and the house that he had built, And the meat of his table, and the sitting of his servants, and the attendance of his ministers, and their apparel, and his cupbearers, and his ascent by which he went up unto the house of the LORD; there was no more spirit in her... And King Solomon gave unto the queen of Sheba all her desire, whatsoever she asked, beside that which Solomon gave her of his royal bounty. So she turned and went to her own country, she and her servants. Both ladies were successful and you can be too. Take the Authority that God purposed for you and use it respectfully. You will be successful in what you do, just remain in your own lanes and your needs will be met."

1 Kings 10:1-13

Let us learn from these ladies, the *Queen of Sheba* sought wisdom over her natural power; and The *Shunamite woman* was graceful in hospitality. As women of God we are capable of making decisions for our future. "For God hath not given us the spirit of fear; but of power, and of love, and of a sound mind" (2 Timothy 1:7).

DIVINELY ARRAYED IN VIRTUOUS BEAUTY

Women of choice for conference *Shipuiah and Puah*, They chose to obey God rather than man; and were divinely arrayed in Virtuous beautiful apparel. There is a necessity for us to remember the precious love of God in many ways. As the saying goes, "we wear many hats as women, there is one for someone in our path to help others in ministries, to become whole by reaching out to the poor both natural and spiritual with love, and kindness for women that fear the Lord, shall be praised in her gates" (Author unknown).

"Many daughters have done virtuously, but thou excellest them all.
Favour is deceitful, and beauty is
vain: but a woman that feareth the
Lord, she shall be praised. Give her
of the fruit of her hands; and let her
own works praise her in the gates."

Proverbs 31:29-31

Puah and Shipuiah refused as chief midwives
to kill all boy babies as ordered by Pharaoh;
being over 500 midwives and appointed by the
Egyptian government, they had to make a decision and they knew to follow their divine teach-
ings. Therefore, they saved the male children
by obeying God, rather than man. "And Samuel
said, Hath the Lord as great delight in burnt offer-
ings and sacrifices, as in obeying the voice of the
Lord? Behold, to obey is better than sacrifice, and
to hearken than the fat of rams" (1 Samuel 15:22).
Puah and Shipuiah are striking witnesses against
the legalized practice of abortion which is going

on in several nations. We must love ourselves
virtuously and help others.

> "And the king of Egypt spake to the
> Hebrew midwives, of which the
> name of the one was Shiphrah, and
> the name of the other Puah: And
> he said, When ye do the office of
> a midwife to the Hebrew women,
> and see them upon the stools; if it
> be a son, then ye shall kill him: but
> if it be a daughter, then she shall
> live. But the midwives feared God,
> and did not as the king of Egypt
> commanded them, but saved the
> men children alive. And the king
> of Egypt called for the midwives,
> and said unto them, Why have ye
> done this thing, and have saved the
> men children alive? And the mid-
> wives said unto Pharaoh, because
> the Hebrew women are not as the

Egyptian women; for they are lively, and are delivered ere the midwives come in unto them. Therefore God dealt well with the midwives: and the people multiplied, and waxed very mighty. And it came to pass, because the midwives feared God, that he made them houses."

Exodus 1:15-21

Women we have beauty within, produced by the experiences we've had, and was able to overcome. *Naomi* nurtured, a woman of grace and courage. She was a great mother, and mother-in-law; her name meant the pleasant one. She was one of noble character.

Naomi is such an innate character that causes one to sympathize with her. She experienced much suffering; and as a young wife had to flee from Bethlehem due to a famine. This was foreign to her; having compassion for people and loving God. Whatever your status in life is, and the things you may suffer; God loves you, sub-mission, and trust in him will pay off. Both her sons were married; regrettably, she mourned the loss of her husband and two sons, but her inner love for her daughters-in-law continued to flourish even though she remained in Moab. God allowed Naomi to look after her daughter-in-law Ruth. We today as women, have some challenges in our families, but staying with the Lord Shows one how to continue life in a positive manner. Ruth was blessed with a husband because of her obedience to God and Naomi. As the Scripture admonishes us, obey God rather than man: "Then Peter and the other apostles answered and said, we ought to obey God rather than men" (Acts 5:29). Put your life in God's hand and he will direct your path; rely on the woman within Appareled *in Virtuous Beauty*.

Celebrating A Decade of Blessings & Embracing A Glorious Tomorrow

Focus: Continuing in Fellowship

In 2008, we culminated with the last *Many Apparels of Women's Conference* in Alaska. Yes, it was a hard thing to understand; but God has a way to use women in his work, if we avail ourselves to him. When He has other plans for you, just be obedient to those who have rule over you and put it in God's hands. If he has a new venture for you it will come to pass.

Since the conference's infancy and throughout the ten year adventure, several of the participants have gone on to begin women conferences to reach the lost, help them to know Christ, overcome hurts, and to receive what God has promised, peace, and life. Remember we are vessels adorned and Suitably fit for kingdom work, let us continue our destinies.

We began this quest with the training sessions with many workshops throughout the tenure of the conference. Emphasis was placed on the inner apparel, and not on what one sees on the outside. In the session, *"I Am woman,"* the importance of *godly Lingerie*, and the challenges of working in close mentoring relationships.

During the session *"Her name is Woman"* we dealt with different women of the bible who had characteristics of different interests to fit a daily situations in women's lives today. This conference focused on the lives of *Leah, Huldah* and *Anna*, women of several different characters. Leah a woman chosen of God but not merely appareled in the natural. A woman whose unhappy marriage, became God's blessings to humanity; we have women today that are going through such situations, but you too can make it.

As I reminisce on another session, *Ages and Stages*, I focused on the life of *Dinah*, a young woman victimized because of immaturity. Let's train our children, mentor them and live a saintly life before them. Teach them the way of a godly woman such as *Lydia a, Christ honoring professional*. So many professionals are in our churches, we are gifted, talented, intellectually astute, well trained and educated. Let's stand in the gap for others that come in contact with. Also, I reference to such a woman as *Jochebad, a caring and nurturing Mother.* She saved the life of her child and God honored her efforts of love and courage. "By faith Moses, when he was born, was hid three months of his parents, because they saw he was a proper child; and they were not afraid of the king's commandment" (Hebrews 11:23). God provided a way for her son to be shielded from the King that wanted to kill the baby boys of that time; and used his daughter to take him to safety in their home. "The LORD said unto my Lord, Sit thou at my right hand, until I make thine enemies thy footstool" (Psalms 110:1).

To prepare for the future there were such trainings and studies that included: ***Knowing Who and who's you are. The Depth of one's Maturity teaches us how to share, ask, and receive help. Learn to walk and work together with the wisdom of God.*** Become and remain Spiritually Dressed for any occasions you might face; ***Study to know the difference, in Church work and Kingdom work*** in order to reach the needy. ***Take authority through Christ in Pursuit of your Destiny.*** The women of today are able to soar far beyond man's expectations, you can be one of them. Keep in mind as we enter the future to array ourselves in *Divine and virtuous Apparel* in order to be identified to the world as who we are, and go forward with a celebrating attitude for tomorrow. There will be no limit to your Aptitude!

Remember "The Many Apparels of Women" we should dress in modest apparel not for great attention but for divine identification and you will, embrace your Future with Confidence. I am assured you were blessed by this book. The Biblical characters, and testimonies will help you battle the storms of life as you work toward purpose and destiny. Know this my sisters, you are not alone! Others have come before you and I have the confidence if they made it, you can also. Know that I am praying for you, as you continue as a successful woman both natural and spiritual through Christ the Lord. Finally, "And they overcame him by the blood of the Lamb, and by the word of their testimony; and they loved not their lives unto the death "(Revelation 12:11). Prayerfully, your testimonies will cause you to become a *World Changer through Christ*.

Let your inward apparels be a replica of who you are, as you embrace your tomorrow.

9 781498 452601